S0-AIV-282

ANIMALS
That Make a Difference!

Dolphins
돌고래

Ashley Lee

Explore other books at:
WWW.ENGAGEBOOKS.COM

VANCOUVER, B.C.

WWW.ENGAGEBOOKS.COM

Dolphins: Level 1 Bilingual (English/Korean) (영어/한국어)
Animals That Make a Difference!
Lee, Ashley 1995 –
Text © 2021 Engage Books
Edited by: A.R. Roumanis
and Lauren Dick
Translated by: Gio Oh
Proofread by: Tamara Kazali

Text set in Arial Regular.
Chapter headings set in Arial Black.

FIRST EDITION / FIRST PRINTING

All rights reserved. No part of this book may be stored in
a retrieval system, reproduced or transmitted in any form
or by any other means without written permission from the
publisher or a licence from the Canadian Copyright Licensing
Agency. Critics and reviewers may quote brief passages in
connection with a review or critical article in any media.

Every reasonable effort has been made to contact the
copyright holders of all material reproduced in this book.

LIBRARY AND ARCHIVES CANADA CATALOGUING IN PUBLICATION

Title: Animals That Make a Difference: Dolphins Level 1 Bilingual (English/Korean) (영어/한국어)
Names: Lee, Ashley, author.

ISBN 978-1-77476-455-8 (hardcover)
ISBN 978-1-77476-454-1 (softcover)

Subjects:
LCSH: Dolphins—Juvenile literature
LCSH: Human-animal relationships—Juvenile literature

Classification: LCC QL737.C432 .L44 2020 | DDC J599.53—DC23

Contents
목차

What Are Dolphins?
돌고래는 무엇인가요?

Dolphins are small
whales with long noses.
돌고래는 긴 코를 가진 작은 고래다.

Dolphins live in groups called pods.
돌고래는 떼라고 불리는 그룹을 지어 살아요.

5

What Do Dolphins Look Like?
돌고래는 어떻게 생겼나요?

The smallest dolphins are Maui dolphins. They are only 5 feet (1.5 meters) long. The largest dolphins are orcas. They can be up to 30 feet (9 meters) long.

제일 작은 돌고래는 마우이 돌고래에요. 길이는 5피트(1.5미터) 밖에 안돼요. 제일 큰 돌고래는 범고래에요. 30피트(9미터) 길이까지 자랄 수 있어요.

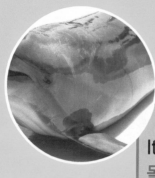

Dolphin skin is smooth. It feels like rubber.
돌고래의 피부는 부드러워요. 마치 고무 같아요.

6

Dolphins have a hole on the top of their heads called a blowhole. The blowhole is used for breathing.
돌고래는 머리 꼭대기에 분수공이라고 불리는 구멍이 하나 있어요. 분수공은 숨을 쉬는데 사용해요.

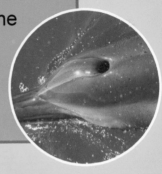

Dolphins have sharp teeth. They have between four and 240 teeth.
돌고래는 날카로운 이빨을 가졌어요. 4개에서 240개의 이빨을 가졌어요.

7

Where Do Dolphins Live?
돌고래는 어디서 사나요?

Dolphins live in shallow water. They need to be able to stick their blowholes out of the water to breathe. Dolphins live in every ocean in the world. Some dolphins live in rivers.

돌고래는 얕은 물가에 살아요. 돌고래는 숨을 쉬기 위해 분수공을 물가에 내놓고 살아야해요. 돌고래는 전세계 바다에 다 살아요. 몇몇 돌고래는 강에 살기도 해요.

Hector's dolphins only live near New Zealand.
Burrunan dolphins live near the Australian coast.
Humpback dolphins can be found near South Africa.
헥터 돌고래는 뉴질랜드 근처에만 살아요. 부르난큰돌고래는
호주 해안 근처에 살아요. 혹등고래는 남아프리카 근처에서
찾아볼 수 있어요.

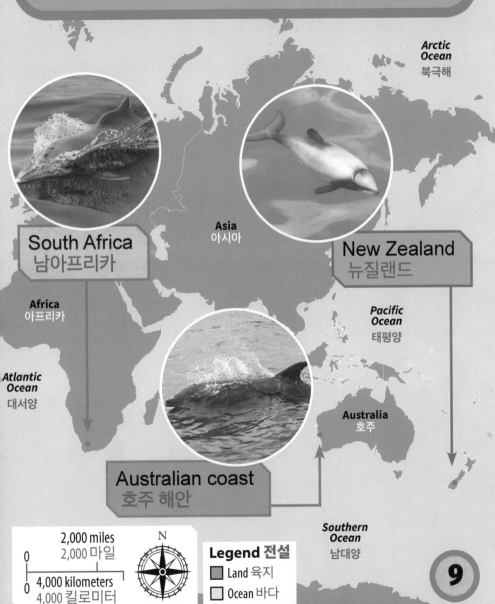

Arctic
Ocean
북극해

Asia
아시아

South Africa
남아프리카

New Zealand
뉴질랜드

Africa
아프리카

Pacific
Ocean
태평양

Atlantic
Ocean
대서양

Australia
호주

Australian coast
호주 해안

Southern
Ocean
남대양

2,000 miles
2,000 마일
0
0
4,000 kilometers
4,000 킬로미터

N

Legend 전설
Land 육지
Ocean 바다

9

What Do Dolphins Eat?
돌고래는 무엇을 먹나요?

Dolphins eat fish and squid.
돌고래는 물고기와 오징어를 먹어요.

Large dolphins eat sea lions or smaller dolphins.
큰 돌고래는 바다사자나 더 작은 돌고래를 잡아 먹습니다.

11

How Do Dolphins Talk to Each Other?
돌고래는 서로 어떻게 이야기하나요?

Dolphins talk using clicks, squeaks, and whistles. Every dolphin has a unique whistle.
돌고래는 딸깍소리,찍찍소리 그리고 휘파람을 사용해 소통합니다. 모든 돌고래는 그들만의 독특한 휘파람 소리를 가지고 있어요.

12

Dolphins find each other using special calls. These calls bounce back to the dolphin when they hit an object. Dolphins hear their calls and can tell where other dolphins are. This is called echolocation.

돌고래들은 특수한 소리를 사용해서 서로를 찾아요. 이 소리는 물체에 부딪히면 돌고래에게 돌아와요. 돌고래는 이 소리를 듣고 다른 돌고래가 어디있는지 알 수 있어요. 이게 바로 반향 위치측정이에요.

13

Dolphin Life Cycle
돌고래의 일생

Baby dolphins are called calves. They have darker skin than adult dolphins.
아기 돌고래는 새끼 돌고래라고 해요. 새끼 돌고래는 어른 돌고래 보다 짙은 피부색을 가지고 있어요.

Calves can travel far with their mother's help. They help them until the calves become strong swimmers.
새끼 돌고래는 엄마의 도움이 있어야 멀리 여행할 수 있어요. 엄마 돌고래는 새끼가 강한 수영선수가 될 때까지 도와준답니다.

14

Calves live with their mothers for 3 to 6 years. Some dolphins will stay in the same pod their whole lives.
새끼 돌고래는 엄마 돌고래와 3년에서 6년을 같이 생활합니다. 어떤 돌고래들은 평생 같은 무리에서 살아간답니다.

Most dolphins live for about 30 years. Some dolphins can live for more than 50 years.
대부분 돌고래들은 30년을 살아요. 어떤 돌고래들은 50년이상 살기도 한답니다.

15

Curious Facts About Dolphins

Dolphins have friends. They prefer to spend time with some dolphins more than others.
돌고래는 친구들이 있어요. 다른 동물들에 비해 돌고래들은 자기들끼리 시간 보내는 것을 더 좋아해요.

Dolphins use tools. They will cover their nose with a sponge while they search the ocean floor for food.
돌고래는 도구를 사용해요. 돌고래는 먹이를 찾아 바다 밑을 살펴볼 때 해면으로 코를 보호해요.

Dolphins can jump 20 feet (6 meters) out of the water.
돌고래는 물위 20피트(6 미터) 까지 점프할 수 있어요.

16

돌고래에 대한 흥미로운 사실들

Dolphins do not chew their food. They use their teeth to catch fish and swallow them whole.
돌고래는 음식을 씹어 삼키지 않아요. 이빨로 물고기를 잡고 통째로 삼켜버립니다.

Some pods are made up of more than 1,000 dolphins. Pods this large are called superpods.
어떤 무리는 1,000마리가 넘는 돌고래들이 있어요. 이런 무리는 대형 무리라고 불립니다.

Dolphins are very smart. They can solve problems and plan for the future.
돌고래는 아주 똑똑해요. 미래 계획을 세우고 문제를 해결 할 수 있답니다.

17

Kinds of Dolphins
돌고래의 종류

Dolphins are related to whales and porpoises. There are about 40 kinds of dolphins. They can be many different colors and sizes.

돌고래들은 고래와 알락돌고래와 관련이 있어요. 40종이 넘는 돌고래들이 있는데 모두 다른 색깔과 사이즈를 가지고 있답니다.

Bottlenose dolphins are one of the most common kinds of dolphins. They shed and regrow their skin every two hours.

병코돌고래는 돌고래중에 가장 흔한 종류의 돌고래에요. 두시간마다 피부를 벗겨내고 새 피부를 만들어냅니다.

18

Orcas are the largest dolphins.
They are also called killer whales.
범고래는 가장 큰 돌고래에요.
범고래는 육식고래라고도 불린답니다.

Amazon river dolphins have long snouts.
Some of the males are pink.
아마존강돌고래는 긴 주둥이를 가지고
있어요. 어떤 수컷들은 핑크색을 띤답니다.

19

How Dolphins Help Earth
돌고래가 지구를 돕는 방법

Dolphins are a sign to humans that an area is clean and healthy. Dolphins will disappear from an area if something is not right.

돌고래가 있다는 뜻은 사람들에게 그 지역이 깨끗하고 건강하다는 말이에요. 그 지역에 무언가가 잘 못 됐다면 돌고래는 사라진답니다.

20

Scientists know that a habitat is in danger if dolphins disappear from it. This can help scientists keep Earth clean and safe.

돌고래가 사라지면 과학자들은 그 서식지가 위험에 처했다는 사실을 알게됩니다. 이 사실 덕분에 과학자들은 지구를 깨끗하고 안전하게 지킬 수 있어요.

21

How Dolphins Help Other Animals
돌고래가 다른 동물을 돕는 방법

Dolphins help animals that are hurt. They will help injured animals to the surface of the water for air.

돌고래는 다친 동물들을 도와줘요. 물 표면 위로 올라가 공기를 쐴 수 있게 다친 동물을 도와줘요.

22

Dolphins keep oceans healthy by eating sick fish. This prevents diseases from being spread to other fish.
돌고래는 병든 물고기를 먹어서 바다를 깨끗하게 지켜줘요. 이는 다른 물고기들에게 병이 퍼지지않게 도와줘요.

How Dolphins Help Humans
돌고래가 사람을 돕는 방법

Dolphins have been known to save humans from shark attacks. They will also find help for people who are trapped in the water.

돌고래는 상어로부터 사람을 지켜준다고 알려져있어요. 또한 물에 빠진 사람을 구해주기도 한답니다.

24

Some dolphins help people catch fish. They guide fish towards fishing boat nets. They are rewarded by eating any fish that escape the nets.
어떤 돌고래들은 사람들이 물고기를 잡을 수 있게 도와줘요. 배의 그물쪽으로 물고기를 몰아준답니다. 그 대신 그물에서 빠져나온 물고기를 먹습니다.

Dolphins in Danger
멸종위기의 돌고래

Many dolphins can get stuck in fishing nets.

많은 돌고래들이 그물에 갇히기도 합니다.

This can injure the dolphins. It also stops them from getting to the surface of the water to breathe.
이 때문에 돌고래는 부상을 입을 수 있어요. 또한 물 위로 올라가지 못해 숨을 못쉬기도 합니다.

27

How To Help Dolphins
돌고래를 돕는 방법

Dolphins eat garbage they find in the water. This can make them very sick.

돌고래는 물 속에서 찾은 쓰레기를 먹기도해요. 이때문에 돌고래는 심하게 아프기도 합니다.

28

Many people are cleaning up oceans
and rivers to help save dolphins.
They are cleaning up garbage and
old fishing nets that can hurt dolphins.
많은 사람들이 돌고래를 돕기위해 바다와
강을 치웁니다. 돌고래를 다치게 할 수 있는
낡은 그물과 쓰레기들을 치워요.

29

Quiz
퀴즈

Test your knowledge of dolphins by answering the following questions. The questions are based on what you have read in this book. The answers are listed on the bottom of the next page.

다음 질문에 답하고 돌고래에 대한 지식을 테스트해봐요. 질문은 책의 내용에 기초합니다. 정답은 다음 페이지 하단에 있어요.

1 Where do dolphins live?
돌고래는 어디에 사나요?

2 How do dolphins talk?
돌고래는 어떻게 말하나요?

3 What are baby dolphins called?
아기 돌고래는 뭐라고 불리나요?

4 How far out of the water can dolphins jump?
돌고래는 물 밖으로 얼마나 멀리 점프할 수 있나요?

5 How many kinds of dolphins are there?
돌고래의 종류는 얼마나 있나요?

6 How do dolphins keep oceans healthy?
돌고래는 어떻게 바다를 건강하게 유지하나요?

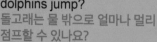

30

Explore other books in the Animals That Make a Difference series.

Visit www.engagebooks.com to explore more Engaging Readers.

Answers:
1. In shallow water 2. By using clicks, squeaks, and whistles
3. Calves 4. 20 feet (6 meters) 5. About 40 6. By eating sick fish

CPSIA information can be obtained
at www.ICGtesting.com
Printed in the USA
LVHW072036120122
708423LV00009B/595